D1552029

At Home in Savannah

Great Interiors

At Home in Savannah

Great Interiors

**PHOTOGRAPHED BY
VAN JONES MARTIN**

**TEXT BY
HARRIS TATTNALL**

ISBN: 0-932958-00-1

Designed by **Van Jones Martin**
Design and Printing Consultant
Douglas M. Eason
Typography by
Copy Grafix
Printed and Bound by
Rose Printing Co., Inc.
Tallahassee, Florida

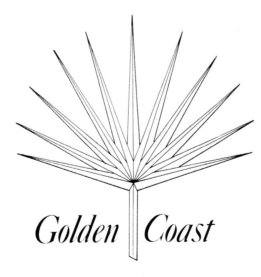

Golden Coast

Publishing Company

CONTENTS

INTRODUCTION: AT HOME IN SAVANNAH   7

24 HABERSHAM   12

510 EAST ST. JULIAN   14

324 EAST STATE The Davenport House   16

206 WEST BAY   21

124 ABERCORN The Owens-Thomas House   22

121 BARNARD The Telfair Museum   29

41 WEST BROAD The Scarbrough House   32

10 EAST OGLETHORPE The Juliette Low House   34

321 BARNARD   39

230 BARNARD   42

325 ABERCORN The Colonial Dames House   44

3 WEST PERRY   48

11 WEST JONES   50

244 EAST OGLETHORPE   52

327 BULL   54

429 BULL   58

15 WEST PERRY   66

17 PRICE   70

212 WEST JONES   72

412 EAST LIBERTY   74

116 WEST HARRIS   75

311 EAST CHARLTON   76

18 WEST TAYLOR   78

225 EAST HALL   81

118 WEST HALL   84

View of Madison Square, 1855.

At Home in Savannah

Buildings are the clothes a society wears, cut to its particular taste and pocketbook, its aspirations and habits. The conservative, dignified and simple rows of dwellings which line Savannah's tree-shaded streets reflect the conservative, dignified and simple life of this nineteenth century city. Savannah was a port of considerable importance during the nineteenth century, but it remained relatively isolated, the southernmost city of consequence on the Eastern seaboard at the brink of a largely unsettled Southern frontier. Though its history was punctuated at times by fires, epidemics, depressions and wars, life in Savannah was regulated by the rhythm of the rising and falling of hot summer suns, the coming of planting and harvest seasons, the arrival and departure of trading ships from England and New England.

Savannah had been established in the second quarter of the eighteenth century on a sandy bluff overlooking the Savannah River. A hundred years later, during the second quarter of the nineteenth century, the river bank was lined with a forest of ships' masts. In January, 1844, there were thirty-five ships in port, coming from or going to Wiscasset, Boston, Providence, London, Dublin, Bordeaux, the West Indies, Philadelphia, Baltimore, Bermuda, Nassau, Darien, but most of them for New York and Liverpool. Light draft schooners followed the coast, darting from port to port. Steamboats went upriver to Macon, Hawkinsville and other cotton markets. The steamboat *Charleston* made weekly trips—"unavoidable delays excepted"—between South Carolina and Georgia, leaving Charleston every Monday and Savannah every Thursday. The trading ships brought cheap, heavy cargo, with some fancy goods for the carriage trade, and sailed away with Southern cotton. Fancy chairs from Boston, Duncan Phyfe sofas from New York, Baltimore stenciled tables, and guava jelly from Havana and linen sheets from Ireland all came to Savannah across the wharfs of the port. The railroad was not completed as far as Macon until 1843.

On the west side of town, between a canal and swampy rice fields, was Yamacraw, a neighborhood of shanties, bawdy houses and saloons, where sailors and blacks spent much time. About 1835, a visitor, surveying the northeast corner of town, could see a grassy slope at the river's edge, the remains of an old earthenwork fortification from the War of 1812, and further down river, he could see a shipyard, a sawmill and cotton press. Playful youths spent idle hours sliding down the loose sandy bluff between the town and the river, for few commercial buildings had been constructed along the promenade which would become Factors' Walk, and the stone ramps and walls at the bluff were not built until the 1840's.

By 1847 the city extended only as far as Liberty Street. Many of the lots at the southern part of town were empty and many lots facing important squares remained unoccupied. Beyond Liberty Street only two buildings were in view. The city common, a wide field overgrown with weeds and grass waist high where boys liked to hunt night hawks in the summertime, began at Harris Street. A pine forest began at the corner of what would become Gaston Street. White Bluff Road, cutting through this dense forest, crossed an open ditch over a wooden bridge. In 1852 this forest was carved into "Forsyth Place" and the ditch and bridge became the site for an elegant cast iron fountain. From the city exchange, a tall building used by merchants and city officials at the river, a watchman was stationed, keeping an eye out for fires. He was ready to sound the alarm with a rapid ringing of a great bell, and he could easily survey the whole town, for it was scarcely a mile square.

Savannah's streets were sandy, muddy in winter and dusty in summer. (The first "paving" came in 1849, when a plank road was constructed down Bay Street and West Broad Street, and in 1871, when Bay Street was paved with asphalt blocks.) At the end of the eighteenth century, the city government hired "an Overseer of the Streets" to cut down weeds in the streets. Horses and mules were a problem throughout the nineteenth century, wandering loose in the streets, and as late as 1881, cows were permitted to lounge in the roads. Hundreds of turkey buzzards kept the streets clean, scavenging for horse manure. Water wagons sprinkled the roads, trying to keep the dust down in hot summer months. Chinaberry trees were planted to decorate and shade the streets during the first thirty years of the nineteenth century. These handsome trees had deep cooling shade and fragrant fruit, which attracted clouds of chattering birds; but their powerful roots damaged wells and foundations. And so during the 1830's the city ordered many of the chinaberry trees chopped down, and in 1839 the city offered to pay $2 to any citizen who would plant and cultivate for two years an oak, wild orange or elm tree. By the mid-nineteenth century, the main streets of the town had avenues of large trees, sometimes four-deep, and sidewalks of planks or bricks.

Public wells were dug in the squares and also at the major intersections, including the corner of Bull and Broughton Streets. Oil lamps were located near each pump, burning whale oil. (The first electric lights were placed in the squares in 1884.) By 1841 there were at least fourteen cisterns and pumps 'round the town. Sometimes horses and wagons were left in the squares against the law. In December, 1809, Mathew Shearer left the mail stage to graze overnight in Johnson Square. The first landscaping of squares began in 1809, when Johnson Square was planted with formal trees, encircled with posts and chains and "two hard walks" were constructed across it. Monument building in the squares began in 1825, when the Marquis de Lafayette dedicated cornerstones for monuments to Nathaniel Greene and Casimir Pulaski, heroes of the Revolution. (Originally there were to be two monuments in Johnson Square and Chippewa Square. However, not enough money could be raised, so in 1830 a single granite obelisk, fifty-feet high, was raised in Johnson Square and dedicated to both men. It was not until the 1850's that a separate monument to Pulaski was erected in Monterey Square.)

Throughout the nineteenth century, most dwellings were box-like structures with simple gable or flat roofs, two stories high over a raised basement, with steps up to a high front porch. A dining room and kitchen were in the basement, two parlors on the first floor, and bedrooms on the second floor. As the century progressed, more and more buildings were built with brick instead of wood, more and more buildings were built as pairs and rows rather than as detached dwellings, and houses were more often three rather than two rooms deep. Though a handful of trained architects designed some splendid houses, most buildings in Savannah were erected by master carpenters, men who copied plans from books or habits learned from apprenticeship. Thus, Savannah houses from 1880 look much like those of 1850, which look much like those of 1820. Old traditions of building, already established, were continued throughout the nineteenth century. Thus, in 1875, an anonymous traveller wrote: "The houses are old-fashioned and stately, having nothing of frivolity of modern style."

Plain people made the best of hand-me-down furniture which their families had brought to Georgia or local slave-made furniture which could be purchased in town, but it was difficult and expensive for even rich people to purchase imported luxuries. Sometimes itinerant goldsmiths, watchmakers, dentists, miniaturists, marble cutters or cabinetmakers, might come to Savannah, looking for a few weeks' work on their way from Charleston, the nearest important city in South Carolina, to Augusta, the closest important city in Georgia. Surely there were a few local cabinetmakers, some of whom probably worked as carpenters and shipbuilders as well. But most household comforts were brought to Savannah by ships from England and New England. The first ice and champagne were imported to Savannah in 1817, books and cloth—from the plainest calico to the richest brocade—were imported from England, rum and other spirits came from the West Indies. Hats, gloves, suits, cravats, dresses, buttons, lace and shoes were usually imported. Coastal traders brought New England windsor chairs, Duncan Phyfe furniture from New York, stenciled Empire tables from Baltimore and Philadelphia.

Most families could not afford to keep horses and simply hired a hack when they needed transportation with luggage or when they were wearing fancy clothes to a party. "Carriage" houses behind dwellings were most often used for storage, servants' quarters and sometimes to house a cow. A new house of 1878 had a pigeon coop and a "henery." A garden might contain nectarines, peaches, apples, plums, pears, apricots, walnuts, mulberries or filbert trees. A lady might purchase fresh flower seeds from England: sweet peas, marigolds, hyacinths, zinnias, sweet Williams, Love-in-a-Puff, Canterberry Bells, poppies, China Pinks, Four O'Clocks, larkspur, hollyhocks, fox glove, marigolds and hibiscus. (Cooking was usually done in basement kitchens and not in outbuildings.)

Days in Savannah began when peddlers, carrying large flat hats which displayed crabs, shrimp and oysters for sale, began to wander the streets at dawn. Until the end of the century the ice man came each morning in his horse-drawn cart. Before the sun rose and the air grew hot, shutters and windows were closed tight to keep in the cool night air. At nine, the master of the household, perhaps accompanied by a servant, walked down to the city market at Ellis Square (where it was located throughout the nineteenth century, except for two years in the early 1820's, when it was moved to Oglethorpe Avenue). It was the man's job to purchase the meat, fowl and staples; it was the wife's job to purchase the vegetables and dainties. Only the poorest family could not afford to hire a cook. After selecting the provisions and giving them to his servant to take home, the master then went to his work; he returned for dinner about two in the afternoon, and went back to work from three to five o'clock.

At dusk, the shutters and windows were opened to let in the cool evening air. After a big dinner in the middle of the day, supper was a simple repast of rice or hominy, fruit and hot tea. Perhaps waiting until a late summer shower had cleaned and cooled the air, the family might promenade down Bull Street and sit around the squares till dark. According to tradition, high class ladies and gentlemen walked only on the west side of Bull Street, while lesser folk stayed on the eastern side of the street. Sometimes a circus would come to town, pitching its tents in the city common; there children could purchase pet chameleons, tied to a tiny chain by a loop 'round their hind legs. Vendors of exotic spectacles—trained animals, wild beasts, magic shows, wax figures, painted panoramas—displayed them at public places. The theater on Chippewa Square, which opened in December, 1818, offered performances at seven o'clock each night; usually there was a double bill, a bawdy farce—"Love Laughs at Locksmiths", "Wild Oats," "The Busy Body"—followed by an uplifting classic or tearful tragedy.

For children, this was a rural world of simple pleasures, taking trips to nearby creeks and marshes to fish and shoot. In April, 1850, George Mercer went hunting over a long weekend at Lebanon, his family farm, and, in spite of bad weather and fear of snakes, he was able to shoot sixteen black birds, three doves, three larks, two partridges, two jackdaws, two night hawks, one snipe, one squirrel, four blue herons, one bittern, two blue peters and a large water turkey, plus several snakes and an alligator. When he went fishing, George could catch shad, sturgeon, mullet, whiting, trout, perch, chub, brim, mud fish, skip jack, jack fish, cat fish, silver fish, croakers, rock fish, bass, sheephead, black fish, flounders, drum, hard heads and eels. Friday nights during the winter were devoted to hunting 'coon and 'possum.

Rivalries were traditional between gangs of boys from the east side and the west side of town. At Christmas, boys from Troup Square always battled boys from Madison Square. One December in the 1890's, Mrs. Meldrim, who lived on Madison Square, hearing the fast approaching shouts of battling boys and fearing that *her* side was being defeated, turned to her butler and said quickly: "Joe, the last battle will be right here in a few minutes. Take down the glass globes from the front door right away!" The winners of these annual battles celebrated victory with a bonfire in Washington Square. Children also played baseball, football, cricket, bandy and shinny in the squares.

For men, too, most pasttimes were athletic. A golf club, jockey club, coit club, rifle club and yacht club had all been established by the early nineteenth century. Virtually all men over the age of eighteen belonged to military companies, which served as social clubs as much as real defense. These companies drilled every Friday night and assembled periodically for tournaments of sabre drilling in Forsyth Park. Other social rites, like the fights and bonfires for children at Christmas, came with the seasons. During the summer, wives and children would take the Central of Georgia railroad to Atlanta and continue by stage to the cool mountains of Hall County at Clarkesville and White Sulphur Springs during July, August and September. Richer families might take steamboats to Virginia or Newport. (Husbands had to stay home, tending to business, except for rare weekends and the summer holiday.) At New Year's Day, ladies dressed in fancy clothes, closed their shutters, lit gas lights, set out refreshments and waited for callers, who came, by rigorous tradition, to pay their respects throughout the day. Gentlemen, usually sharing a carriage in groups of six or eight, would tour the city, street by street and house by house, calling on all the girls they knew. Some groups started at Bay Street and worked south, others started at Gaston Street and worked north. In 1858, Charles Olmstead made 120 such calls on a single day!

Social customs, amusements and many values have changed since the nineteenth century. Our world is busier, noisier, harder, faster. But in Savannah, we are reminded continually of the conservative, dignified and simple life of the nineteenth century. Here, a living city in an historical setting, the most enlightened preservationists are trying to preserve not merely old buildings but a structure of humane, civilized and stable values, which are represented by the buildings themselves. Sometimes these wonderful old houses are spit-and-polished with bright brass and mahogany furniture, sometimes they are untidy with children's toys and littered clothing. In the pages of this book, you will look inside houses with museum quality period rooms and others with informal, contemporary furnishings. But, always, twentieth century people have made themselves at home in nineteenth century Savannah.

24 Habersham

John Mongin's house was built in 1797 and moved to its present site from an adjacent corner, facing Warren Square, in the late 1960's. Though handsomely refurbished with many of its original elements like the finely detailed cornice on the facade, the building has been greatly changed, because it was rebuilt on lower foundations with new front doors and new front porch. Nevertheless, the interiors are among the most beautiful—and the most beautifully decorated—in Savannah.

The Dining Room of the Mongin House, like the Parlor, has a substitute mantle and restored cornice. The Georgian dining table and Queen Anne chairs are English. The mirror, at left, is mid-nineteenth century American.

In the Parlor of the Mongin House, the mantle piece is a replacement—but from another Savannah house of the same period. The dentil cornice reproduces the original, fragments of which survived. The mirror, sofa and candelabra are all English Regency.

BELOW: The back porch, used for meals in the cooler months and midday naps on hot summer days, looks out onto one of the most delightful gardens in the city.

510 East St. Julian

The Parlor of Oddingsells Cottage is filled with a comfortable assemblage of fam
possessions and stylish antiques, including the small Georgian wine stand, left-center, t
small cabriolet Hepplewhite sofa, center, and early nineteenth century work table, far rig

Charles Oddingsells, a planter, built this cottage about 1798-99, one of only a handful of documented buildings which have survived from the eighteenth century in Savannah. Its steeply pitched roof, shed dormer windows, low foundations and wide clapboards are representative of the architecture of that era.

The Guest Bedroom of Oddingsells Cottage is nestled under the gable of the attic and is lit by dormer windows. Though furnished with great simplicity, the architecture makes this a most interesting room.

324 East State

ABOVE: The front and rear of the Hall of Davenport House was divided by a screen on Ionic columns, supporting a segmental arch. The door under the stair leads to a back porch and garden. The tall case clock on the right descended through a distinguished Savannah family and is probably Southern in origin. The elaborately inlaid mahogany fold-top game table on the left is English.

LEFT: The Parlor of Davenport House was decorated, almost boastfully, by its owner-designer with high style architectural ornaments chosen from popular builder's handbooks and catalogues to demonstrate his skill. The Hepplewhite chairs and sette, although undocumented, are probably American. The lady's portrait over the mantel, of Miss Brailsford, was made by Jeremiah Theus, "limner of Charles Town," when he came to Savannah in the early 1770's. The chandelier was given by the National Trust for Historic Preservation.

17

In 1821 Isaiah Davenport, a carpenter and builder from Rhode Island who had come to Savannah at the end of the eighteenth century, built a house for himself on Columbia Square. Trained by experience as an apprentice and not by formal school like a modern architect, Davenport was a conservative master builder who copied the work of others, which he had seen in his youth or in books. So his house, architecturally-speaking, looks back to the simplicity of Georgian England and Federal New England, despite its late date. The building, threatened with demolition for a parking lot, was saved by Historic Savannah Foundation in 1956 and has been open to the public as a house museum since 1962.

The Small Bedroom of Davenport House, seen through the tall posts of the bed, has a William and Mary chest-on-stand, an English wingchair and a delightfully off-center fireplace. The delicate coverlet was made in 1820.

The Dining Room of Davenport House is ready for desert or light refreshments, with two handsome wine glasses at each place. The Hepplewhite dining table from England is finished with simple, tapered legs. The sideboard is American, probably from Virginia. The Chippendale chairs appear to be English. The mantle is a replacement.

ABOVE: The Master Bedroom of Davenport House, like other rooms here, is filled with a comfortable mixture of English and American furniture and decorative arts, no single object a preposessing example but all contributing to an harmonious whole. The bed is American from the first quarter of the nineteenth century, the chest is English from the end of the nineteenth century, and the wing chair is modern.

LEFT: This small Nursery, beside the Master Bedroom, contains a quilt made at Brunswick, Maine, in 1849 and an Italianate cradle made at New York in 1855.

206 West Bay

William Taylor built his warehouse at the west end of Bay Street about 1816, and it survives as the oldest surviving commercial building on the bluff of the Savannah River. Its walls of rough ballast stone, chinked with an odd assortment of leftover bricks, are a reminder of the port's earliest trading days. The warehouse was converted into a modern residence in 1973.

A gigantic wooden wheel, originally used to lift heavy loads from the ships of the river to the bluff of the town, has been used as a dramatic focus for this remarkable conversion. It hangs, like a primitive chandelier, over the stairway and dominates the dining and living areas below and the more informal family area above.

In the Parlor of the Richardson House, the architect has given a square room the appearance of a domed, circular room by making Greek key fretwork circles in the ceiling. The settee was made in 1815 by Duncan Phyfe, the famous New York cabinetmaker. The painting over the mantel by William Etty shows Ann Jay, sister of the architect, painted in England before 1816. The banjo clock was made in Roxbury, Massachusetts, by Aaron Willard. The desk (which looks like a chest because its writing surface is disguised by a drawer), also from New York, is notable for its richly-figured mahogany veneers and brass lion head handles. The chandelier is English, made about 1810.

124 Abercorn

William Jay, a young architect working in London, designed this mansion in 1817 for Richard Richardson, a merchant, banker and promoter. It was already under construction when Jay reached Savannah in December, 1817. The house was completed the following year, a sophistocated blend of classical motifs passed to America by Renaissance Italy and Regency England. Often called the Owens-Thomas House (for the names of later owners), it is open to the public as a house museum operated by the Telfair Academy.

The Entrance Hall of the Richardson House, like other buildings designed by Jay in Savannah, is decorated with sumptuous classical ornament, here egg-and-dart mouldings at the ceiling, a screen of gilt-capped Corinthian columns, a deep baseboard painted to resemble marble, rich paneling and plasterwork.

The Richardson House Dining Room is equipped with a fine dining table and the twelve original chairs made to be used with it, attributed to be the work of Henry Connelly of Philadelphia. The table was used in Savannah throughout the nineteenth century and, indeed, may have been sent to Savannah on a coastal ship for a rich custormer when it was new. Houses all along the coast of the Old South were filled with luxurious commodities and decorations from Baltimore, Philadelphia and New York, brought to port cities by coastal traders.

The Music Room of the Richardson House, which may at one time have been a family dining room, contains the single most important piece of furniture in the house, a settee (properly called a *meridienne*) made by Duncan Phyfe of New York about 1815. Unlike many objects merely attributed to that master craftsman, this settee is completely documented and its mate is in the collection of the Metropolitan Museum. Note the crisp carving on the back rail, imitating swags of soft cloth, the brass feet in the form of lion paws and the graceful reeded legs. The pianoforte was made by Stoddard of Boston in 1826. The rug is an Aubusson.

ABOVE: An arched bridge, which connects the front of the house with the rear in the upstairs hall, is a source of wonder in the Richardson House. Its details imitate the design of the lower stair, with mahogany, iron and brass inlay worked together ingeniously.

BELOW: The first floor room which now serves as a Bedroom of the Richardson House was probably used originally as a parlor. Nevertheless, the room is handsomely furnished with a New York four-post bed, made about 1815, decorated with an especially handsome nineteenth century coverlet. The round table, with its marble top, hairy paw feet and stenciled decorations, was made in New York about 1840.

The second-floor Bedroom of the Richardson House, viewed from the pillow of a four-post English bed, shows a small sewing table attributed to Duncan Phyfe. The gentleman's portrait in the corner was made by Jacob Eicholtz of Lancaster, Pennsylvania. Below it sits one of the famous Staffordshire figures of Benjamin Franklin, mislabeled "Washington," made about 1825. The black bench, stenciled with gold decoration, was made in New York, part of a set in the house.

ABOVE: The rear porch of the Richardson House looks over the beautifully maintained garden to the carriage house behind.

BELOW: The Kitchen of the Richardson House, like most kitchens in Savannah, was located in the basement and not in a separate out-building. The cupboard on the left is a pie safe. It is enclosed by perforated tin panels which served as a screen to allow cooling air in but kept out nasty flies. It was probably made in Georgia during the second quarter of the nineteenth century. The hutch table in the center was made in South Carolina and belonged to the Heywards, one of the great planter families of that state.

121 Barnard

William Jay designed this mansion for Alexander Telfair, the son of an early Georgia governor, in 1820. Its austere exterior is relieved by a portico with Corinthian columns, elaborate cast iron balconies of massive size, and a large demilune window in the hall. Since 1886, the house has served as the Telfair Academy of Arts and Sciences, the oldest art museum in the Southeast.

The Long Gallery of the Telfair House was originally divided into two parlors by a screen of columns. When the building was converted into an art museum in the 1880's, the columns were removed. Now this gallery is filled with pictures, furniture and decorative arts from America and England during the late eighteenth and early nineteenth centuries.

A close look at the front of the Long Gallery of Telfair House shows the rich cornice, heavy mouldings, carved marble mantles and inset arches of William Jay's original architecture. The desk was made in England at the end of the eighteenth century; a rolling, tambour top covers the writing surface when not in use, and the bell-flower inlay decorating the legs is notable. A copy of the 1754 first edition of Thomas Chippendale's famous *Cabinet Makers Directory* is displayed on the desk. The *meridienne* and chair, both of maple, were probably made in Philadelphia about 1825.

"And a little child shall lead them" is inscribed on this panel on a mantel in the Long Gallery. It was carved by John Frazee, probably in New York, about 1818, and it is typical of the classical and biblical inspirations for mantel decorations of Federal period houses, including those by William Jay.

The Dining Room of Telfair House is filled with original Telfair family furniture, including the large round dining table, maple chairs and gilt-embellished sideboard. The chairs, inspired by designs from classical Greece, reflect the spirit of late Federal and early Greek Revival America. The sideboard, although Empire in style, has been attributed to Duncan Phyfe, whose career extended from the end of the eighteenth century well into the Empire period.

41 West Broad

William Jay designed a mansion for William Scarbrough, merchant and promoter of the steamship *Savannah*, in 1819, completed just in time to entertain President James Monroe when he visited Savannah in that year. The archaic Doric columns and heavy entablature of the portico dominate the exterior. A dramatic entrance hall, a classical atrium two stories high, surrounded by a balcony supported by four more massive Doric columns, dominate the interior. The house is being restored by Historic Savannah Foundation as its headquarters.

The Entrance Hall, shown on this and the facing page, was restored after years of abuse and neglect. Because evidence of the original design was confused or missing, some parts of the restoration—the skylight, second-floor plasterwork and the staircase (not rebuilt)—are conjectural. Just as the original architect, Jay, often copied other buildings he had seen in England, the restoration architects of the 1970's copied the designs of English houses of Jay's time. The sofa, sideboard and chairs are of the American Empire style.

10 East Oglethorpe

The home of James Moore Wayne, a lawyer who later became a justice of the U.S. Supreme Court, was built in 1821. William Jay may—or may not—have designed this building. Some experts say he designed it, then moved to Charleston, sending a builder back from South Carolina to supervise the work. Other experts say the house is simply the work of another designer, who copied some of Jay's architectural devices. The third floor was added in 1886 for a later owner. The Girl Scouts of America have restored the house as a monument to its founder, Juliette Gordon Low, who was born there in 1860.

The Parlor of Wayne House is dominated by the portrait of Juliette Gordon Low, copied from the original by Edward Hughes, now in the National Portrait Gallery, Washington. The wonderful Empire sofa, with gilt decorations and carving in the form of eagles and dolphins, was made in New York about 1825. The Gothic Revival side chair, sitting at the window to the left of the fireplace, would have been made between 1835-50.

ABOVE: The Rear Parlor of Gordon House is seen as an entertainment center with reading, music, and stereoscope viewing. The portrait of Eleanor Kinzie is by Juliette Low from the original by George Peter Alexander Healy. The landscape over the 1820 Sheraton spinet is "Niagara Falls by Moonlight," a souvenir from the Gordons' honeymoon.

ABOVE LEFT: The stairway of Wayne House.

LEFT: The Dining Room of Wayne House, decorated with cut glass and pink azaleas, is ready for company. The dining table, originally designed with a pedestal base in the 1850's, has been cleverely alterred—by adding new tapered legs with spade feet—to imitate the earlier Hepplewhite style and also to make the table more sturdy! The table, like many other furnishings in the house, belonged to Juliette Gordon Low's parents. The chairs are nineteenth century versions of the Chippendale style.

ABOVE: The Bedroom of W.W. Gordon, father of Juliette Low, a cotton factor in Savannah who earned the rank of General during the Spanish-American War. His portrait, painted about 1910, hangs above the mantle, which appears to have been added in the 1850's.

LEFT: Mrs. Gordon's Bedroom is furnished with the bed in which Juliette Gordon Low was born in 1860. The bed was part of Mrs. Gordon's *trousseau*.

Bernard Constantine, a butcher and merchant, built his house facing Pulaski Square in 1845. With its gable roof, raised basement, high front porch and side hall plan, it is typical of the architecture of its period. After years of neglect, it was restored with special care in 1971-2.

321 Barnard

The Parlors of Constantine House, connected by wide sliding doors, contain similar furnishings—dark mahogany case pieces, Chippendale armchairs upholstered in the same green-and-gold flamestich, Empire mirrors and two Portuguese needlework rugs. In the front parlor, the secretary is English from the third quarter of the eighteenth century. The wooden mantels have been marbleized. The superb ceiling medallions are original.

ABOVE: The Guest Bedroom of the Constantine House has a large maple bed from
South Carolina, made in the second quarter of the nineteenth century, a small pine work
table from Virginia and a handsomely patterned Portuguese rug.

ABOVE: The Porch of Constantine House is modern, designed to reproduce the details of the original front porch and the spirit of nineteenth century Savannah. From the porch an afternoon visitor, iced tea or mint julep in hand, can overlook the green garden and a panorama of old houses in the neighborhood.

LEFT: The Dining Room and Library of Constantine House look out into a green garden of grass and boxwood. In the Library, the wing chair, fruitwood and mahogany Hepplewhite armchairs and the double-fronted partners' desk are all English. The rug is Portuguese needlework.

230 Barnard

Charles B. Cluskey, an architect who came to Georgia from Ireland during the 1830's, designed this house for Aaron Champion in 1844. A third floor was added in the 1890's. Like other houses designed by Cluskey, this house has a dramatic projecting portico, massive columns and classical motifs moulded in stucco.

LEFT: The Entrance Hall of Champion House is perhaps the most dramatic architectural space in Savannah, in which two screens of square columns frame an oval hole in the ceiling, which looks up three stories to a sky light. The robust mouldings and marble floor make a very rich effect.

The Parlor of the Champion House is a delightful mixture of English furniture of many complementary styles, including a small Chippendale sofa and armchair, a Queen Anne tea table, a Hepplewhite wing chair and side chair, a tapestry-covered Hepplewhite stool in the French taste and two small Chinese tables.

325 Abercorn

John S. Norris, who came to Savannah from New York in the late 1840's, designed this house for Andrew Low, an English-born cotton merchant, in 1850. Like other houses Norris designed in Savannah during the 1850's, this building combines various styles in a virtuoso display of the eclectic spirit—the wide-bracketed eaves and romantic garden of the Italian Villa Style and the entrance columns and chaste plan of the Greek Revival. The house is now operated as a house museum by the Colonial Dames.

The Parlors of Low House, shown in two views, are furnished with complementary English and American eighteenth and nineteenth century antiques. The pair of *meridiennes*, probably made in New York or Philadelphia between 1830 and 1850, are fine examples of their type. The small drop-leaf table, ready for serving tea, with its brass inlay and hairy paw feet and turned colonettes, could be the work of Michael Allison of New York.

This small Bedroom of Low House, with its handsome but austere Greek Revival mantel, reminds us that famous visitors have spent the night here, including Robert E. Lee and William Makepeace Thackeray.

The Dining Room of Low House, infused with a golden afternoon light which amplifies the colors of the walls and curtains, is equipped with comfortable English furniture, not at all inappropriate for the home of an English-born merchant.

The Front Parlor of the Thompson House is filled with wonderful *pairs* of objects: two gilt Georgian consoles at the windows, two Georgian chandelabra on them, two Hepplewhite sofas, two small Empire ebony tables, two Hepplewhite armchairs in the French taste, two small velvet footstools. The hypnotically patterned floor was laid in the late nineteenth century.

3 West Perry

This house is like a person who has lived three lives! Built in 1831 by Joseph R. Thompson as a simple gable-roofed frame dwelling with a side hall plan, the house was greatly enlarged in 1839 when a new owner, James J. Waring, a famous local physician and later mayor of Savannah, added six new rooms—which made the side hall into a central hall and doubled the size of the house. Finally, in 1874 the house was completely remodeled in Renaissance Revival style.

The Rear Parlor of the Thompson House has an early nineteenth century pianoforte from Boston, an imposing Queen Anne lacquer cabinet with Chinoiserie decoration, a Regency sofa from England and, partly hidden behind the fireplace, a portrait of Robert E. Lee, in uniform.

11 West Jones

Joseph Johnston built this house in 1854, with the local grey bricks, high stoop and long windows so typical of buildings in Savannah at that era. Behind this traditional exterior is hidden one of the most dramatic renovations, architecturally-speaking, in Savannah.

ABOVE: The Parlor is lined with an apricot *moiré* silk, intended as a high Victorian effect. The armchair to the right of the modern sofa is an expecially fine Regency one with spoon-back and Greek key fretwork.

LEFT: The Dining Room was enlarged with a dramatic, vividly-angled, glass-sheathed addition in 1977.

Mary Marshall constructed four row houses (actually two pairs of double houses) on Oglethorpe Avenue, facing Colonial Cemetery, in 1855. These wonderful buildings, with marble-sheathed front steps leading to unusually spacious parlor floors, handsome grey bricks of local manufacture and tall, wide windows, are fine examples of paired and row houses from mid-nineteenth century Savannah.

The Dining Room in Marshall Row is hung with a hand-painted French wallpaper, which reproduces an early nineteenth century design, "Promenade de Josephine," and depicts views of the island of Martinique. The two mantels are Belgian and replace the originals, which have been stored for safekeeping. The visible furniture is English. The Hepplewhite chairs, carved with sheaves of wheat, are upholstered in gold velvet.

Oglethorpe

327 Bull

The Hall of the Green House has a floor of ceramic tiles imported from England, a ceiling of ribbed square panels with foliated decorations, and marble-topped consoles. On the left is a library, stair and dining room; on the right, two parlors facing Madison Square.

The Stair of Green House ascends at a right angle from the front hall to a domed well, lit by a skylight during the day and by a circle of gas jets at night.

John S. Norris designed a house for Charles Green, an English cotton merchant, in 1853. It is the most important example of the Gothic Revival in Georgia, set apart from all other buildings in Savannah by its exotic, exuberant decoration and by the opulence of its costly materials. In December, 1864, General W.T. Sherman used the house as his headquarters, when the U.S. Army occupied Savannah at the end of the Civil War. Now the parish house for St. John's Church, the house, often called the Green-Meldrim House, is open to the public several days each week.

The Parlors of the Green House, seen here and on the following page, retain important original fittings, including the gigantic gilt mirrors over each mantle, the gas chandeliers and wall jets. The mahogany door frames, the fanciful plasterwork arches and ornaments, and the massive cornice express the ambitions of both the owner and designer of this extraordinary building.

429 Bull

John S. Norris designed this house for General Hugh Mercer in 1860. Left incomplete during the Civil War, its timbers were removed by U.S. soldiers to make shelters in Monterey Square during their occupation of the city in 1864-65. The house was completed in 1869. Like other buildings designed by Norris, it is an expression of the eclectic spirit, combining various details of Greek Revival, Italian Villa and Renaissance Revival styles.

The Hall of Mercer House is floored with English ceramic tile, similar to those in the Green House, and the stair ascends, like the Green House, to a domed skylight. The bronze sculpture from France, dating from the nineteenth century, depicts Pluto coming out of hell. The portrait of the gentleman, also French, was painted 1815-20.

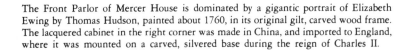

The Front Parlor of Mercer House is dominated by a gigantic portrait of Elizabeth Ewing by Thomas Hudson, painted about 1760, in its original gilt, carved wood frame. The lacquered cabinet in the right corner was made in China, and imported to England, where it was mounted on a carved, silvered base during the reign of Charles II.

PRECEDING PAGES: In the Center Parlor of Mercer House hangs a vast Flemish tapestry, made about 1730, which depicts Diana cavorting with nymphs. The two armchairs, upholstered in their original needlepoint covers, were made in France at the middle of the eighteenth century. The portraits of two Philadelphia sisters were painted by Henry Benbridge. The gilt table with cabriolet legs covered with rococo ornament is from Scotland.

ABOVE: In the Rear Parlor of Mercer House, a portrait of Lord Coyningham by James McNeil Whistler, seen over the mantle, and Aubudon prints by Havell hang on the walls. The mantel was removed from an early nineteenth century Savannah house.

RIGHT: The Dining Room of Mercer House is decorated with a pair of portraits by Thomas Hudson, painted in Bristol, hanging above a cabinet used to store silver, on the left, and a two-tiered cellerette, used to store wine, on the right. The dining table is from England, made in the early nineteenth century, and the chairs are from Scotland, also made in the first quarter of the nineteenth century. The silver, bearing her royal monogram, belonged to Queen Alexandria, consort of Edward VII.

ABOVE: The Study of Mercer House contains a nineteenth century replica of an eighteenth century French *bureau plat*, which once belonged to a Mexican emperor. The painting over the mantle shows George Drummond of Scotland by Gainsborough Dupont, nephew of the famous Thomas Gainsborough. The pembroke table beside the wingchair was made in Savannah by Thomas Elfe, Jr. The mantel was removed from the Mongin House, built in 1817 in Savannah.

RIGHT: The Bedroom of Mercer House has a New York high post bed, made in New York about 1825-30, and a cheerful early nineteenth century chest from New England. The mirror is early eighteenth century, with a walnut veneer and carved pine, gilt decoration. In the adjacent dressing room, we can see a richly figured Empire chest from New York or Philadelphia with lion face handles.

15 West Perry

Like many other Italianate buildings in Savannah built during the late 1860's, this house, completed in 1867 for John Stoddard, was probably conceived, designed and perhaps begun before the Civil War. Though not documented, this house has been attributed to John S. Norris, the most important architect working in Savannah during the 1850's.

Without sacrificing architectural integrity, the Living Room has been revived with cheerful colors, a vivid carpet, and many pots of plants and trees. Five prints by Mark Catesby, an eighteenth century English naturalist who came to territory which would later become Georgia, hang above a Chippendale sofa on the left.

ABOVE: The Dining Room, connected by wide, sliding doors with the living room, has the same colors and profusion of green plants, as well as fine English chandelier and demilune sideboard.

BELOW AND RIGHT: An enlarged Kitchen and Breakfast Room of the Stoddard House has been created by extending the rear of the house and enclosing the back porch.

The Porch has been enclosed with glass walls. Looking out into a
walled garden, lined with ferns and shady trees, it is a perfect
place for breakfast in the morning or reading in the afternoon.

Originally built in 1857 for Elizabeth Heery, this simple dwelling has been much abused, considerably alterred and recently enlarged. Having once been used as a corner market for slum dwellers at its saddest time, the recent adaptation of this building represents the renewal of old Savannah during the last twenty years, two decades during which hundreds of decayed slum dwellings have been brought back to life by patient and caring families.

17 Price

In the Living Room, some family furniture, a discreet sense of style, and a few new architectural ornaments around the doors and windows have brought to life an otherwise undistinguished space. The Empire sofa, with its hairy paw feet, and the mahogany tray, mounted on a modern stand, create an atmosphere of hospitable comfort.

The Parlor is contemporary in detail but classical in spirit, with the plain white plaster walls and simple furnishings. The dramatic sculpture over the mantel is by Martin Schriber of New York, the lithograph between the windows by Phillip Sutton of England, and the walnut cocktail table by a craftsman in Kentucky.

212 West Jones

Elizabeth, Isaac and Jacob Cohen built this house in 1852. Originally a simple, frame dwelling with a gable roof, the building was enlarged in 1872 by adding the mansard roof and lengthening the windows on the front parlor floor. Its renovation demonstrates how comfortably a completely modern interior can fit into the skin of an historic building.

412 East Liberty

This house was one of eight dwellings designed as a row in 1883 for Nicholas and Mary Jones. In the early 1970's, a young architect gutted his house and redesigned the interior to create a lively and personal living space. It is worth noting that the simplicity of most nineteenth century Savannah dwellings lend themselves happily to this contemporary treatment, especially when the exterior—as here—has been treated with respect.

An enlarged Parlor was created by the designer for this narrow house. Removing the original stair hall allowed more room for living; replacing the original double door between parlors allowed more wall space where it was badly needed.

Since David Turner built this house in 1846, it has been alterred somewhat later in the nineteenth century by enlarging the door and front porch and adding a small wing. Restored by a young lawyer with children, today the building shows how living in an old house can be fun for the whole family.

116 West Harris

The Family Room in the basement of Turner House is filled with comfortable—and indestructable—family furnishings, country baskets woven in South Carolina, cheerful, brightly-pattered fabrics and two fireplaces.

Mary Edmundson built her house on East Charlton Street in 1873. In later years, the original high stoop was removed and the front door relocated at the street level.

311 East Charlton

ABOVE: A corner of the Kitchen, hung with native baskets and cooking gear, is set for breakfast.

LEFT: The Family Room has been stripped of all its original plaster to reveal the raw brick on the walls and naked beams of the ceiling.

18 West Taylor

This tall, narrow house was built in 1913 for Andrew L. Farie. The interior has been reorganized, most inventively, to create a three-story courtyard through the center of the house, by removing the interior rooms and leaving a glass-walled passageway between the front and rear rooms. This treatment is especially appropriate for a house of relatively recent construction.

The Living Room, looking out through sliding glass doors into a plant-filled, brick-lined terrace, is private without begin confined.
The plain plaster, light colors and modern furnishings continue the exotic mood that is much in keeping with the subtropical climate.

18 West Taylor—Continued

The Courtyard is formed by the space between the front and rear room which are linked by a two-story passageway on the right.

BELOW: The Bedroom is a cool, and very comfortable, expression of modern design in a rehabilitated nineteenth century dwelling.

William Gibbons Preston of Boston designed this house for George Baldwin in 1888. Preston was the most important architect working in Savannah during the late 1880's, most often designing in the spirit of H.H. Richardson's Romanesque Revival with bright red bricks, terracotta, cast iron, dark paneling and assymetrical plans and profusion of exotic ornaments.

225 East Hall

The Parlor of the Baldwin House has been furnished with comfortable family chairs and a sofa, which, happily, fit perfectly the mood and period of the house.

ABOVE: The polygonal Library of the Baldwin House is equipped with records and books and comfortable English club chairs from the nineteenth century, a ceiling fan (not original), and stained glass window (which is).

RIGHT: The Entrance Hall of the Baldwin House, at once classical and romantic in spirit.

118 West Hall

Alfred S. Eichberg, an architect from Atlanta who had been born in New York and worked in Savannah during the 1880's and early 1890's, designed this house for J.P. Williams in 1883. Eichberg was one of those eclectic late nineteenth century designers who devised buildings which used many different styles and intricate motifs, including turrets, towers, spindles, brackets, stained glass—which were at once an appeal to the romantic spirit and the triumph of factories and machinery in late nineteenth century America.

The Dining Room of the Williams House is furnished with a pedestal dining table, Chippendale side chairs and a massive Empire sideboard, accompanied by standing lamps heavy with the mood of the 1920's.

The Parlor of the Williams House, seen in two views, has been furnished with a happy hodgepodge of comfortable, modern furniture, exotic Oriental tables, Chinese export porcelain, English antiques and palm trees—perfectly suited to the flamboyant and exuberant spirit of the house.

ABOVE: The Study of the Williams House, a small room off the entrance hall, is an extremely personal assortment of old photographs, collectibles, Tiffany glass and slip-covered furniture.

RIGHT: The Hall of the Williams House is an expansive, almost baronial, room, with a large fireplace surrounded with dark oak paneling, orange and blue stained glass, beamed ceiling and wildly assymetrical plan.

The Bedroom of the Williams House, with its tall mid-nineteenth century mahogany bed, dark panneled walls, sporting paintings, landscapes and satin quilt, successfully creates an aura of masculine grace.